D1208962

SEA OTTER HEROES

THE PREDATORS THAT SAVED AN ECOSYSTEM

PATRICIA NEWMAN

MILLBROOK PRESS • MINNEAPOLIS

FOR KEN, MY FIRST READER AND
PATRON OF THE ARTS

Author acknowledgments: I'd like to thank Brent Hughes, David H. Smith Research Conservation Fellow, University of California Santa Cruz & Duke University, and Lilian Carswell, the Southern Sea Otter Recovery & Marine Conservation Coordinator, US Fish and Wildlife Service, for introducing themselves to me at that long-ago conservation scientists retreat on Tomales Bay. Their enthusiasm for Brent's scientific discovery, the Elkhorn Slough, and of course, sea otters was contagious. They generously gave their time for interviews, shared their photos with me, and provided thoughtful comments on numerous manuscript drafts. Additionally, I'd like to thank Elise Newman for accompanying me to Elkhorn Slough on a mother-daughter adventure. Many of her photos can be found in these pages.

Millbrook Press
A division of Lerner Publishing Group, Inc.
241 First Avenue North
Minneapolis, MN 55401 USA

For reading levels and more information, look up this title at www.lernerbooks.com.

Main body text set in Avenir LT Pro Roman 13/18.
Typeface provided by Linotype AG.

LIBRARY OF CONGRESS CATALOGING-IN-PUBLICATION DATA

Names: Newman, Patricia, 1958– author.
Title: Sea otter heroes : the predators that saved an ecosystem / Patricia Newman.
Description: Minneapolis : Millbrook Press, [2017] | Audience: Ages 8–12. | Audience: Grades 4 to 6. | Includes bibliographical references and index.
Identifiers: LCCN 2016020573 (print) | LCCN 2016029400 (ebook) | ISBN 9781512426311 (lb : alk. paper) | ISBN 9781512428445 (eb pdf)
Subjects: LCSH: Sea otter—Juvenile literature. | Seagrasses—Ecology—Juvenile literature. | Marine habitats—Juvenile literature. | Marine ecology—Juvenile literature. | Elkhorn Slough (Calif.)—Ecology—Juvenile literature.
Classification: LCC QL737.C25 N49 2017 (print) | LCC QL737.C25 (ebook) | DDC 599.769/5—dc23

LC record available at https://lccn.loc.gov/2016020573

Manufactured in the United States of America
2-45425-23323-2/13/2018

CONTENTS

A JOURNEY BEGINS

WHAT DOES A PLAYFUL SEA OTTER HAVE TO DO WITH FLOWERING SEAGRASS THAT GROWS UNDERWATER? While they share an ocean home, one is a mammal and the other is a plant. One eats crabs and fish. The other uses photosynthesis to make food. One frolics in the sea. The other sways to an underwater rhythm.

But in fact, a critical link between the two exists, a link that marine biologist Brent Hughes found completely by accident. Finding that connection solved a scientific mystery that Brent had almost given up on.

From a young age, Brent enjoyed figuring out the "how" and "why" of marine life. "I had only visited the ocean a handful of times as a kid," said Brent, who grew up in Kansas, more than 1,000 miles (1,609 kilometers) from the nearest ocean. "But I spent a lot of time near the Great Lakes. I was drawn to

Scientists Brent Hughes *(right)* and Lilian Carswell motor up the Elkhorn Slough. Brent relied on Lilian's sea otter expertise during his research.

Sea otters usually forage in the morning and evening and rest in the middle of the day. Rest time includes grooming. Well-groomed fur traps air between its layers to keep otters warm in cold water.

water, and was always out in nature exploring and trying to catch fish, worms, and insects."

After studying biology in college, Brent traveled to the Oregon coast for graduate school. There he discovered the Pacific Ocean's intertidal zones: areas close to shore where the tides wash in and out. Brent describes intertidal zones as a beautiful mosaic of habitats. "They are home to a diverse community of plants and animals," he says. "They provide the food *and* a place to live." Intertidal zones benefit people in several ways too, such as protecting the coastline from rough weather. Brent's curiosity kicked into gear. He had to know more about these fascinating environments.

As he continued his graduate studies, Brent focused on one specific intertidal area called Elkhorn Slough (pronounced *slew*), an inlet of Monterey Bay, in Northern California. The long, narrow slough is an estuary, where freshwater from nearby creeks and rivers mixes with salt water from the ocean. Pelicans, harbor seals, and sea otters thrive. Thick meadows of seagrass grow among the sand and rocks below the surface.

The twisting slough borders the farms of the Salinas Valley, which grow acres and acres of strawberries, artichokes, brussels sprouts, lettuce, celery, tomatoes, spinach, and broccoli. Known as America's Salad Bowl, the valley produces most of the United States' salad greens. Many of these fields are only steps from the water, and they have a direct effect on the health of the slough.

"Elkhorn Slough is one of the most nutrient-polluted estuaries on the planet," Brent says.

Sea otters sleep, eat, and groom while floating at the water's surface.

Pickers with large bags strapped to their backs harvest vegetables on a Salinas Valley farm.

Farmers spray chemical fertilizers on crops to help them grow strong and fight off disease. Then rain and regular watering rinses the fertilizer off the plants and into nearby streams, rivers, and eventually the ocean. This runoff contaminates the waterways with extremely high levels of nutrients, which can disrupt the balance of marine ecosystems—the plants and animals in a habitat.

Brent discovered that Elkhorn Slough didn't react like most nutrient-polluted waters. Usually the excess nutrients encourage large amounts of algae to grow. The algae coat each blade of seagrass and prevent the grass from performing photosynthesis. Without photosynthesis the seagrass can't grow and reproduce, so it dies. And because of the important roles seagrass plays in the environment, our air quality, coastlines, and fishing industry suffer. "But the seagrass in the slough was healthy and lush and green," Brent says. "It didn't make sense, but it was fascinating. This seagrass thrived, and in theory it should not."

In Elkhorn Slough, seagrass floats just below the surface of the water. The healthy, bright green color surprised Brent.

Why did the seagrass flourish?

Brent was determined to find out. But his journey to discovery would zigzag like the slough itself, requiring crafty detective work, the scientific method, and a smidgen of luck.

CHAPTER 1

THE MYSTERY UNFOLDS

TO BRENT, THE HISTORY OF THE SLOUGH IS AS FASCINATING AS ITS SEAGRASS MYSTERY. About eighteen thousand years ago, a glacier carved out the slough's channel. When the glacier retreated, or melted, salt water surged in to take its place. Freshwater from nearby rivers also flowed in, bringing sediment with it—bits of sand and rock that settled on the estuary floor. These sediments eventually formed the muddy banks of the salt marshes that border the slough. "The Elkhorn Slough was part of a vast tidal network of estuaries in the Salinas River valley," Brent says. "It used to be massive."

Over the last two hundred years, as the area became more settled, the size of the slough shrank. Southern Pacific Railroad laid tracks in 1872 that separated eastern portions of the slough from the saltwater tides. From the 1880s to the 1940s, farmers and ranchers dried out land for fields and pastures by digging ditches and building dikes to hold back the tides. In 1908 a winter storm with strong waves moved huge amounts of sediment and closed the mouth of the Salinas River, north of the slough. The same storm opened a new mouth a short distance south, causing the river to bypass Elkhorn Slough. That eliminated the slough's largest source of freshwater. And in 1946, the US Army Corps of Engineers dredged an area next to the Pacific Ocean to form Moss Landing Harbor. Each of these events changed the slough's size, its shape, or the ratio of freshwater to salt water. The present-day slough is only 7 miles (11 km) long.

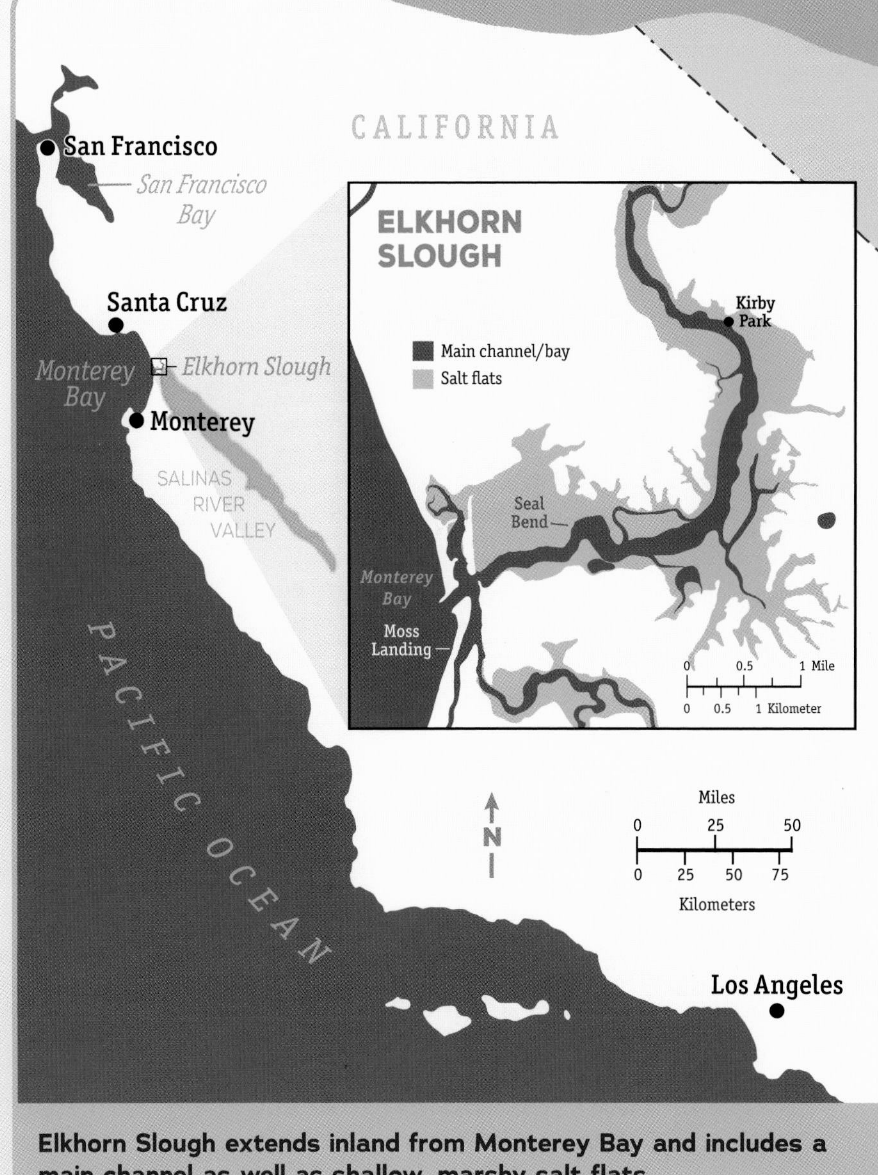

Elkhorn Slough extends inland from Monterey Bay and includes a main channel as well as shallow, marshy salt flats.

Moss Landing is a small fishing town popular with tourists and marine research scientists. Moss Landing Harbor acts as a gateway between Monterey Bay and Elkhorn Slough.

Understanding the estuary's history motivated Brent and scientists like him to protect and preserve this rich, vulnerable ecosystem. Harbor seals ride the incoming morning tide after a night of hunting and then snooze in the sun at their favorite spot on the muddy banks. Sea otters float on their backs to devour fat crabs or groom themselves before a nap.

About one hundred species of fish use the estuary too. Anchovies, sardines, flatfish, jellies, bat rays, octopuses, and leopard sharks catch a ride into the slough on cold, clear tidal waters from the bay. Clams and crabs burrow into the salty mud. "Some of them are residents, but some of them use the estuary as a nursery—a place to grow up," Brent says.

OTTERISMS

MISTAKES OF THE PAST

Many years ago, sea otters almost disappeared forever. Their brush with extinction began in the fall of 1741 when a group of Russian explorers became shipwrecked. The explorers' small ship floundered on the storm-tossed waters of the northwest Pacific Ocean just east of Russia's Kamchatka Peninsula. The terrified men aboard battled violent winds, bitter cold, and a lack of freshwater and food. Finally, the rough sea deposited the ship on an island. Small brown sea otters peered at the visitors, and their curiosity became their undoing. At first, the men ate birds and seals, but eventually the men ate the otters too.

By August 1742, the Russians had built a new vessel and set sail for home. Georg Steller, the ship's naturalist, wrote, "From November 6, 1741 to August 17, 1742 we killed more than 700 of the animals, consumed them, and took their pelts along to Kamchatka."

For the next 168 years, from the Bering Sea to the Aleutian Islands and down the coast of North America, hunters from Russia, Great Britain, and the United States clubbed, speared, and shot sea otters for their valuable pelts. By 1830 so few animals remained that hunters could no longer earn a profit, and the hunt petered out. Finally, the 1911 International Fur Seal Treaty and a 1913 California law banned sea otter hunting. Were these protections too late? Many people thought sea otters were already extinct.

In 1915 the lighthouse keeper in Big Sur, California, shared some good news. "Sea otters are increasing, at least around Point Sur the last two years," he wrote. About the same time, a Monterey, California, resident counted thirty-two sea otters while driving down the coastal highway. Since then sea otters have experienced a slow recovery thanks to strong legal protections. As their population expanded, some otters swam north and entered Elkhorn Slough. The slough protected them from large sharks and provided a plentiful food supply. The number of sea otters in the slough continues to increase.

Fur traders examine fox and sea otter pelts in this 1902 illustration.

A pelican *(top left)*, a harbor seal *(top right)*, and a great egret *(bottom)* are all at home in the slough.

The variety of fish also draws more than 340 species of birds to the estuary. Great blue herons ambush their prey by standing motionless until a likely meal swims by. Snowy egrets perform a ballet in the shallows to scare up a snack. Pelicans with large throat sacs soar above the water scanning for unsuspecting fish and then dive beak-first with a tremendous splash when they spot one.

Healthy seagrass supports much of this wildlife. It grows in underwater beds throughout the slough, approximately 6 to 15 feet (1.8 to 4.6 meters) below the surface at high tide. At low tide, the long, smooth blades of seagrass rest on the surface. Above or below the water, the blades use sunlight to change carbon dioxide and water into plant food through photosynthesis. As seagrass makes its food, it gives off oxygen, enriching the slough.

SEAGRASS SCIENCE

HOW SEAGRASS WORKS FOR US

Seagrass provides four important services for its ecosystem and for the planet:

1. It dampens currents and waves. Calmer waters protect our coastlines from erosion and rising sea levels. "Imagine a giant seagrass meadow in front of a little beach with a bunch of homes," Brent says. Without seagrass, crashing waves would erode the beach little by little, and the water might eventually flood the homes.
2. It provides a nursery habitat for young marine life. Among seagrass blades, the young find food, places to hide, and protection from predators, harsh tides, and weather. "The fish come in as juveniles, grow really fast, and then head out to the bay as adults," Brent says. "That's why we call it a nursery." Some common seafood species such as salmon, Dungeness crab, and herring spend part of their lives in a seagrass bed.
3. It traps farmland sediments laced with pesticides that flow into the slough. "The grass buries the contaminants before they travel to the open ocean [and harm wildlife]," Brent says.
4. Seagrass meadows excel as one of four ocean ecosystems that store excess carbon from the atmosphere. Together with kelp forests in cold water oceans, mangrove forests (aquatic trees) in the tropics, and salt marshes (which border the Elkhorn Slough and other estuaries), seagrass absorbs carbon and locks it away in its roots, where it's buried forever. Plants that remove carbon from our environment ease the effects of climate change.

Seagrass calms waves along the shoreline in the slough. Despite its grassy appearance, seagrass is not a true grass, because it flowers.

Before each boat trip into Elkhorn Slough, Brent checks the fuel level and oil pressure prior to starting the engine.

To study the seagrass mystery, Brent began exploring the slough by boat in 2011. He usually launched the boat from Kirby Park, near the northeastern end. He would back the boat trailer down the ramp, unfasten the tie-down straps, and push a blue fiberglass skiff off the trailer. The boat looked more like a bathtub than a speedboat, but to Brent, it was home on the water. Most days the sun was warm and the breeze mild in this northern tip of the slough.

Perched on the edge of the skiff, Brent scanned the rippled water. The steady hum of the skiff's motor announced his presence. A tap-tapping occasionally echoed over the water as sea otters cracked open clams and mussels on stones—or sometimes on the hull of Brent's boat.

As Brent traveled closer to the ocean, the breeze picked up and the temperature

Brent inspects a blade of seagrass *(above)*. He finds some brown algae *(right)*, but overall the seagrass looks surprisingly healthy.

dropped. Sometimes a damp fog blocked the sun, and a light chop rippled the surface. The tides gently lift and lower the water in the protected estuary, instead of the violent crashing seen in more exposed areas.

Although seagrass grows underwater, Brent could easily identify the grassy meadows at high tide by looking at the surface. Seagrass calms wave action and currents, so the water directly over it looks glassy smooth. Brent would cut the motor and lean over the side of the boat to pull up a fistful of seagrass. He draped the blades over the side of the boat. Because the slough has some of the highest nutrient levels recorded around the globe, the seagrass here should have been nearly dead. Some of the blades were slimed with brownish algae, but most were silky clean and felt smooth like satin ribbon.

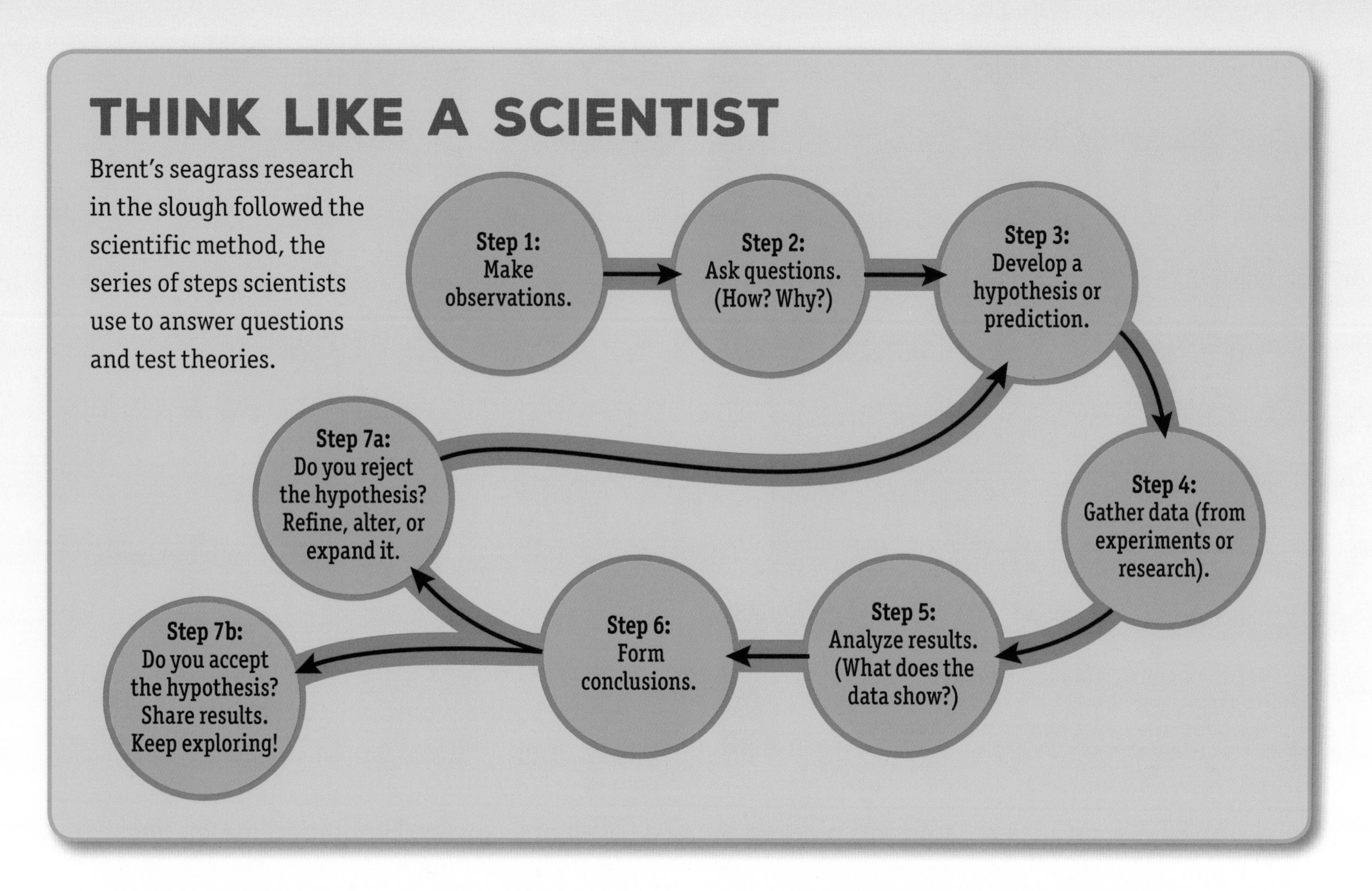

Brent inspected the algae-slimed blades. Nutrients from the Salinas Valley agricultural fields create algal blooms in the water, "kind of an algal feeding frenzy," as Brent describes it. The algae can glom on to the seagrass and prevent sunlight from reaching the leaves. Eventually the grass dies.

In Elkhorn Slough, though, the grass seemed to be able to stay ahead of the choking algae. A closer look at the green blades revealed a key player: well-camouflaged, jellylike sea hares. These fat

Brent holds a blade of seagrass as a sea hare swims away from it.

sea slugs crawl up and down each blade of grass, slurping up algae. Brent calls them lawn mowers, because they keep the seagrass clean.

So Brent added sea hares to his list of clues. He noticed that slough sea hares were bigger and more abundant than in other seagrass ecosystems around the world. Bigger sea hares would obviously gobble up more algae. But he wondered why so many lived in the slough. Perhaps something in the estuary allowed more of them to survive. Finding out why, he thought, might also unlock the mystery of the seagrass.

CHAPTER 2

THE "AHA" MOMENT

LIKE ANY GOOD DETECTIVE, BRENT KNEW THAT HIS SUCCESS DEPENDED ON THE INFORMATION HE GATHERED. First, he decided to take a closer look at the history of Elkhorn Slough seagrass. Lucky for Brent, the slough is a well-studied environment. He turned to scientific data gathered long before he was born. "For me it's really important to put together a picture of what's happening over time," Brent says. Aerial photographs from nine decades showed seagrass coverage in the slough. "We can see from the photos how the habitat has changed in both the seagrass and the marsh vegetation," he says. "When agriculture really started taking off, we saw a big decline in seagrass. But in the 1980s, we saw a complete reversal."

In this aerial view of Elkhorn Slough, seagrass beds appear as brown patches under the blue water.

To find out the cause of this surprising reversal, Brent needed to compare seagrass coverage with other things happening in the slough at the same time. He called on Eric Van Dyke, an expert mapper with the Elkhorn Slough National Estuarine Research Reserve. Eric started with aerial photos from the 1930s. He drew boundaries around the seagrass beds, which looked like dark smudges under the water. These boundaries allowed him to measure the area of seagrass in each photo. Eric generated a spreadsheet for Brent with two columns: the year and the quantity of seagrass measured for that year.

Brent created a graph that showed a simple picture of seagrass abundance over time.

"I'm a visual person," he says. "I look at the trends."

SEAGRASS SCIENCE
SCUBA DIVING

Marine scientists scuba dive to get close to the habitats or animals they study. (Scuba stands for "self-contained underwater breathing apparatus.") Brent *(right)* went on many dives to study seagrass, always floating above it. "If we walked about and trampled it, we would damage it," he says.

Budding marine scientists must earn an entry-level diving certificate before taking a scientific diving course. The course can include one hundred hours on the physics of diving, diving emergency first aid, dive rescue, and several supervised dives.

Next, Brent developed a list of hypotheses, or assumptions, to explain why seagrass in Elkhorn Slough seemed to thrive despite the high level of nutrients. He thought perhaps other seagrass ecosystems in the region thrived too, so Brent compared his data with nearby estuaries. "I collected data on seagrass abundance from places such as Tomales Bay, Humboldt Bay, San Francisco Bay, and Morro Bay to look at their trends," Brent says. But his findings didn't match what he'd seen in the slough. "Some of these [seagrass] populations are crashing. Some of them are stable. Elkhorn Slough is the only one going up."

Brent's second hypothesis suggested that weather patterns, such as El Niño and rainfall amounts, might explain the health of the seagrass. "El Niño drives storms that can wreak havoc in these coastal systems," he says. And El Niño's warm water currents could stress seagrass, a cold-water-loving plant.

On the other hand, milder El Niño storms flush away the algae accumulating on seagrass. Brent compared the dates of the El Niño storms against his seagrass data, but he found no correlation. Mild or severe storms did not correspond with a change in the slough's seagrass. Likewise, rainfall and water temperature differences did not explain the health of the seagrass either.

Brent also briefly considered upwelling from Monterey Bay's deepwater canyon as a factor. When winds push away warm surface water, cold water from deep in the ocean wells up to replace it. The cold water brings vital nutrients to California's coastal waters, which improves the health of plant and animal life. But the Elkhorn Slough is overloaded with nutrients, so this hypothesis fizzled before it started.

Still the mystery lingered.

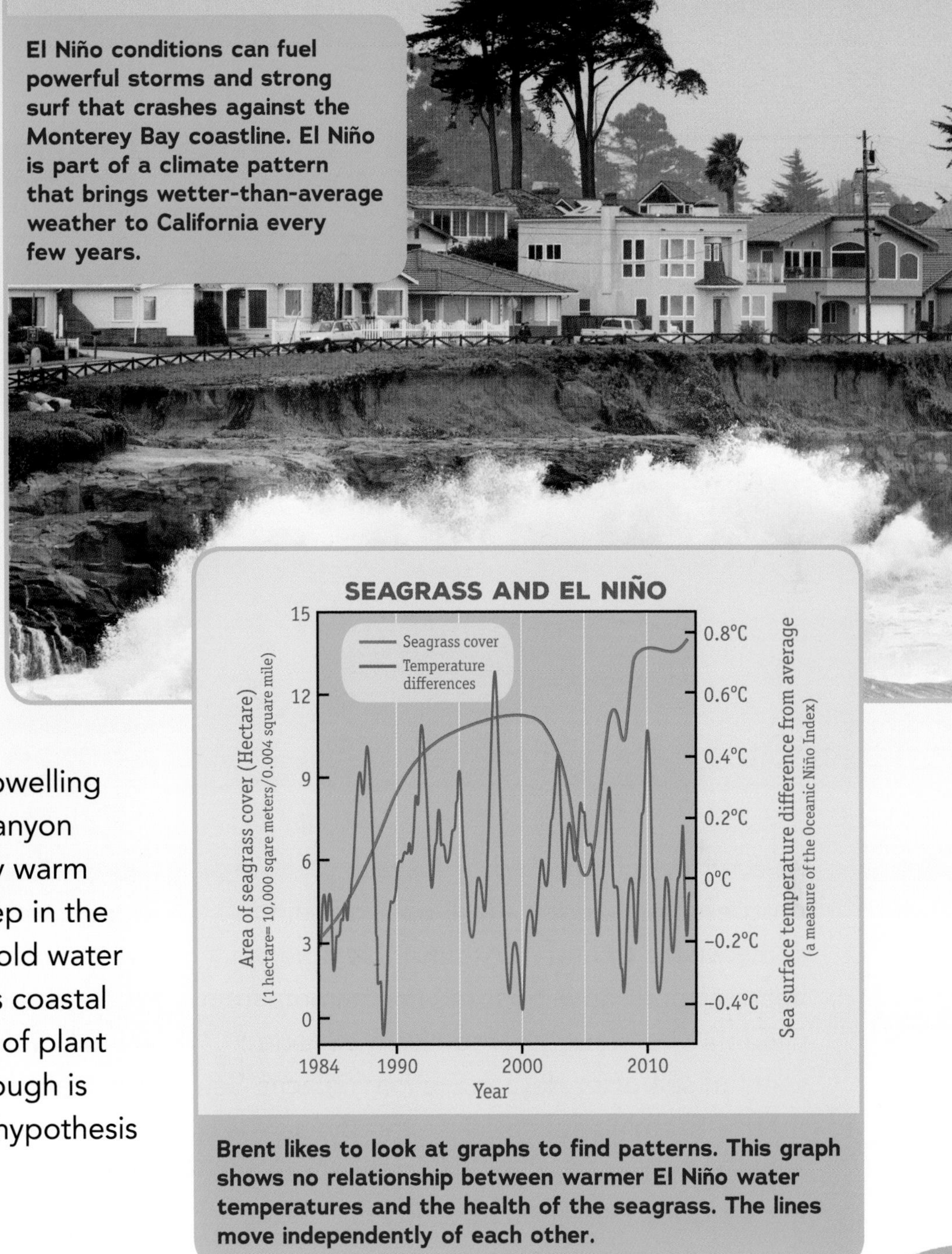

El Niño conditions can fuel powerful storms and strong surf that crashes against the Monterey Bay coastline. El Niño is part of a climate pattern that brings wetter-than-average weather to California every few years.

Brent likes to look at graphs to find patterns. This graph shows no relationship between warmer El Niño water temperatures and the health of the seagrass. The lines move independently of each other.

Ever since sea otters arrived in the slough, tourists have come to see them. But wildlife viewing carries responsibilities. Boats and kayaks must stay at least 50 feet (15 m) from sea otters.

Brent was frustrated by his lack of progress. He needed more data but didn't know where to find it. Around this time, he heard about a tour boat captain named Yohn Gideon who had gathered nearly sixteen years of sea otter data in Elkhorn Slough. Sea otters? Brent was skeptical, even though he'd observed large numbers of otters feeding in the seagrass beds he was studying. "I was a complete disbeliever [that the otters could significantly affect seagrass]," Brent says. But he had nothing to lose.

Captain Gideon had opened Elkhorn Slough Safari in 1995. Adults and children equipped with cameras and binoculars boarded his pontoon boat in Moss Landing Harbor near the Pacific Ocean. Captain Gideon handed a clicker to some passengers, assigning each one a species of wildlife to count. Every sighting equaled one click. Some passengers counted loons or raptors. Others counted geese, ducks, seals, or sea otters.

As the boat motored up the channel, Captain Gideon and a naturalist who joined each tour told the story of the slough, pointed out wildlife, and shared fascinating facts. Throughout the 10-mile (16 km) round-trip, camera shutters and counters clicked. The naturalist later transferred the counts to data sheets with the date and time of the tour and the high- and low-tide levels.

When Brent took a look at the sea otter data, Elkhorn Slough Safaris had compiled more than twenty binders stuffed with data sheets from as far back as 1996. The huge amount of data allowed Brent to graph a trend line. He compared it to his seagrass data.

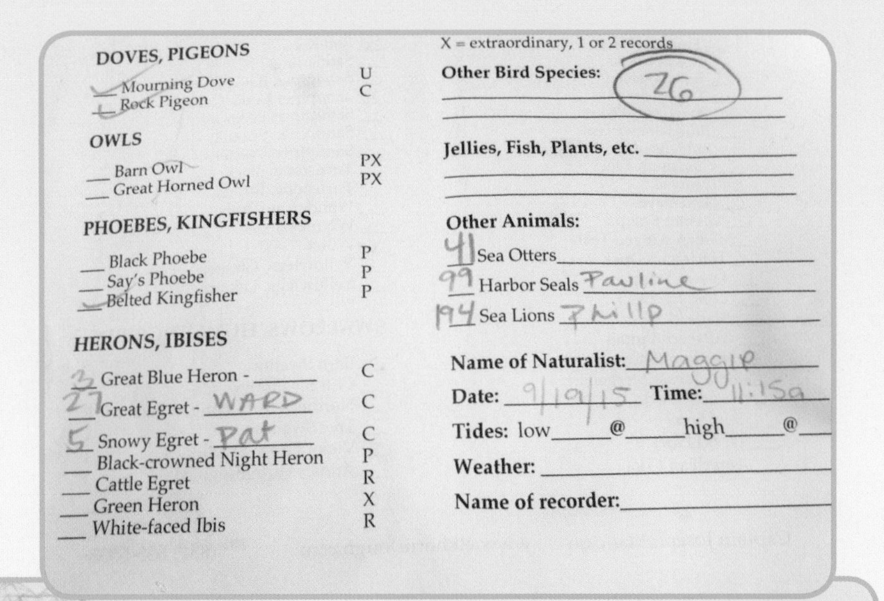

DOVES, PIGEONS

✓ Mourning Dove U
✓ Rock Pigeon C

OWLS

__ Barn Owl PX
__ Great Horned Owl PX

PHOEBES, KINGFISHERS

__ Black Phoebe P
__ Say's Phoebe P
✓ Belted Kingfisher P

HERONS, IBISES

3 Great Blue Heron - ______ C
27 Great Egret - WARD C
5 Snowy Egret - Pat C
__ Black-crowned Night Heron P
__ Cattle Egret R
__ Green Heron X
__ White-faced Ibis R

X = extraordinary, 1 or 2 records

Other Bird Species: 26

Jellies, Fish, Plants, etc. ______

Other Animals:

41 Sea Otters ______
99 Harbor Seals Pauline
194 Sea Lions Phillip

Name of Naturalist: Maggie

Date: 9/19/15 **Time:** 11:15a

Tides: low ____ @ ____ high ____ @ ____

Weather: ______

Name of recorder: ______

A data sheet *(above)* records how many birds, sea otters, and other animals were counted on one boat trip through the slough in 2015. Passengers on Elkhorn Slough Safari tours have helped count wildlife there since 1996.

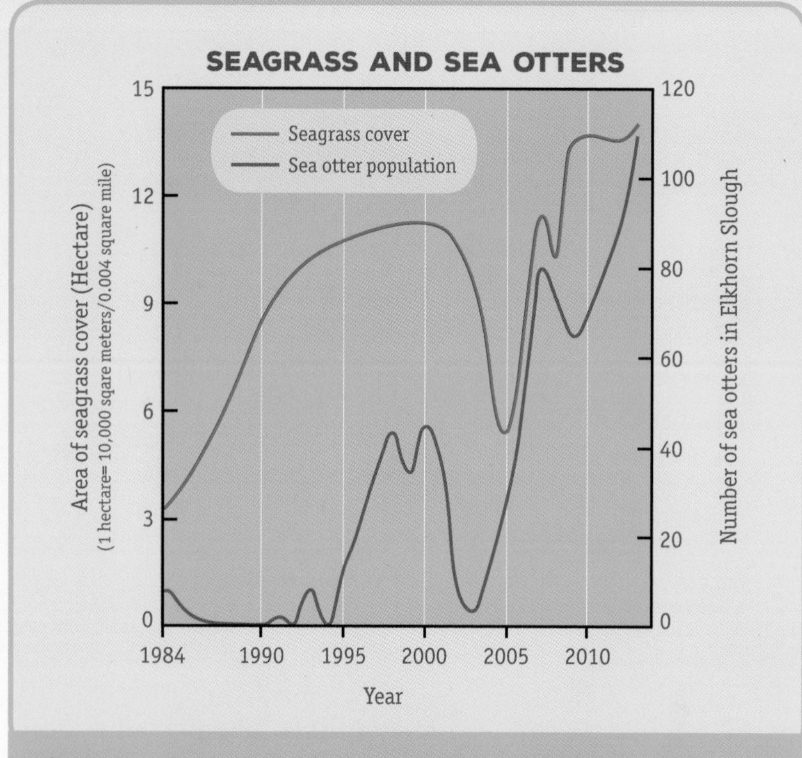

These two lines rise and fall together, suggesting a correlation between sea otter numbers and seagrass health.

"I overlaid Yohn's data with the seagrass data, and it fit together like a glove," Brent says. Otter sightings had risen and fallen in sync with seagrass abundance. "I'm like, what the heck. . . ?"

Clearly, sea otters were somehow linked to seagrass health. But could the otters, apex (top) predators in the protected slough, actually be responsible for the thriving seagrass?

The question thrust Brent into a vigorous scientific debate that had been raging for years. Did forces at the bottom of the food chain, such as nutrient levels, control seagrass health? Or was it controlled by the presence of a predator at the top? Brent had always approached ecology from the bottom up, focusing on how nutrient levels and physical conditions such as storms, waves, and temperatures affected the health of the ocean. Accepting the idea that sea otters helped seagrass would change his entire perspective. He would have to admit that both the bottom *and* the top of the food chain had power over a marine ecosystem.

Before Brent could be sure of his discovery, he needed proof. Captain Gideon's data would not stand up to scientific scrutiny, because it was not gathered with the scientific method in mind. Brent decided to design an experiment to test for himself whether sea otters really improved the health of seagrass. But first, he had to brush up on the habits of his prime suspects.

OTTERISMS

BUILT TO HUNT

CHAPTER 3

PROOF!

EVERY GOOD DETECTIVE NEEDS TO BE FAMILIAR WITH HIS SUSPECTS' HABITS. Where in the slough do sea otters spend time? What do they eat? The design of Brent's experiment depended on the answers to these questions.

Sea otters first entered Elkhorn Slough in 1984. Ever since then, scientists have observed and photographed them. The slough's small area and shallow water make otter spotting easy, compared to studying animals such as sharks that swim in vast stretches of ocean. In the slough, sea otters and their pups are safe from rough waves, killer whales, and great white sharks. The slough makes finding food easier too. A sea otter needs to eat about one-quarter of its body weight in food every day.

Diving, cracking shells, and the constant struggle to stay warm use a lot of energy. Every bite becomes precious. The slough's shallow waters make for short dives, which burn less energy.

Brent contacted fellow scientists to see if they had recorded where sea otters gathered over time. He began with Tim Tinker of the US Geological Survey, who leads sea otter research in California. Tim works with scientists and volunteers from a variety of agencies and organizations, such as the California Department of Fish and Wildlife, the US Fish and Wildlife Service, and the Monterey Bay Aquarium. For one study, Tim and his team attached identification tags to

In the open ocean, otters sometimes fall victim to killer whales *(below)* and great white sharks. However, these large predators more frequently eat sleek, fat-rich seals.

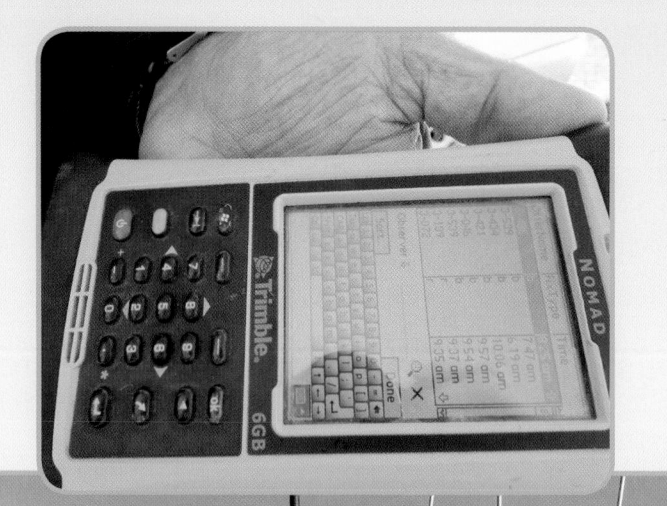

Otter spotters carry handheld receivers *(above)* when on the job. Experienced spotters can log data quickly. *Below:* These otter spotters carry an antenna to pick up the sea otter's transmitter signals.

the flippers of about twenty sea otters. They also surgically implanted very high frequency (VHF) radio transmitters in the otters' abdominal cavities.

Each transmitter sends a signal with a radio frequency assigned to a single otter. Trained trackers, or otter spotters, tune their receivers to each frequency to locate individual otters from onshore or in a boat. Otter spotters then record data about an otter's location and whether it is foraging, grooming, or resting. Using that data, Tim Tinker and his team confirmed for Brent exactly where otters spend their time in the slough.

Tim also shared information about sea otter eating habits with Brent. He and fellow researchers from Monterey Bay Aquarium had simply watched what the otters brought to the surface.

"A sea otter is one of the only predators that dives down, grabs its prey, brings it up to the surface of the water, shows it to you, and then eats it," Brent says. Otter spotters use the otter's paw as a ruler to estimate the size of each prey eaten. Data from ten thousand foraging bouts showed that Elkhorn Slough sea otters ate big, meaty crabs 50 percent of the time.

A sea otter dives for food among kelp fronds in Monterey Bay. In the slough, shallower water means otters spend less energy diving.

Brent considered how the otters' preference for crabs might affect seagrass. He developed a hypothesis. Crabs eat sea hares—the bigger the crab, the more it eats. And sea hares feast on the algae that grows on seagrass. The second part of his hypothesis said that Elkhorn Slough seagrass thrived because of sea otters. It was time to design an experiment to test these ideas. He needed to examine how the elements of the food chain interacted with one another to solve the mystery.

Brent's experiment would have two parts. In part 1, he built miniature seagrass habitats called mesocosms (*MEE-zoh-coz-ums*), a common lab technique that re-creates nature in a bucket, a barrel, or a tank. In part 2, he ventured into the slough.

The design phase for part 1 took Brent about two weeks. Careful planning helped him avoid errors that might ruin his results. When he had a sound design, he gathered twenty large plastic buckets bearing colorful hardware store logos. He set them up in an outdoor study area at Long Marine Laboratory, at the University of California, Santa Cruz, where he was working toward his PhD.

Next, Brent needed to add residents to his mini-habitats. He and his research team boarded their bathtub-like skiff and motored to various seagrass beds. Wearing wet suits, masks, and air tanks, they dove beneath the surface of the slough. They collected shoots of seagrass, sea hares, crabs of different sizes, and sediment. The scientists stuffed the samples into yellow mesh dive bags clipped to their belts before transferring them to coolers on the boat. They used coolers filled with iced water "to keep the organisms as happy as possible," Brent says, before they transplanted the samples into the mesocosms.

Back at the lab, Brent and his team transferred the coolers to wet tables—large, flat sinks with continuously flowing seawater. The samples sat for twenty-four to forty-eight hours on the wet table to get used to their new home. Brent wanted to be sure they survived the stress of the move.

In this mesocosm, seagrass has been transplanted in sediment. The sea hares and crabs have not yet been added.

Ocean animals and plants need seawater to survive. Brent's lab pumps 1,000 gallons (3,785 liters) of water per minute from the ocean and stores it in two huge blue towers. This seawater runs through the tubes in his mesocosms. Overflow is pumped back to the sea.

Two sea hares feed on algae on seagrass. Brent calls the sea hares cryptic because they blend in with the seagrass so well.

Over the next four days, Brent added the same ingredients into each of his twenty buckets—sediment, seagrass, sea hares, and crabs—but the quantities of each were carefully controlled. Brent planted the same weight and number of seagrass shoots in each bucket.

Next, he added sea hares. He had previously measured sea hare numbers in the estuary to figure out how many to add. "The mesocosms have to scale up to the natural world," he says. "We found about eighty sea hares per square meter in the wild, so we used the same ratio to seed our buckets."

Brent inserts a small crab into a mesocosm.

For the next two levels of the food chain, each mesocosm needed a crab and a sea otter. Clearly, sea otters weren't going to fit inside the buckets. So Brent developed an ingenious way to pretend they were there.

Brent had learned that sea otters prefer to eat big, meaty crabs—they eat the biggest crabs first. He reasoned, then, that a seagrass bed with sea otters would have more small crabs than large crabs. On the other hand, in an otter-free seagrass bed, crabs would have the chance to grow larger, so the bed would have more large crabs than small crabs. Therefore, Brent added one small crab to some buckets to indicate that sea otters "lived" there. He added one large crab to other buckets to mimic an otter-free habitat. It may sound backward, but small crabs meant otters were present and large crabs meant otters were absent.

For thirty days, cold seawater flowed into each bucket from a hose over the rim. A drain system captured overflow water and sent it back to the ocean. Brent trained a team of college student volunteers to examine the mesocosms every day and record their observations. They stuck their hands inside each bucket and gently moved seagrass blades to count sea hares. "It's okay if the sea hares reproduce or if algae grow," Brent told them. "It's mimicking the natural world."

At the end of the experiment, Brent and his team spent several days harvesting the ingredients in each of the twenty mesocosms. They carefully weighed the seagrass, the crabs, the sea hares, and the algae that had grown.

Prior to weighing the seagrass, Brent and his team dried it in a food dehydrator. The dehydrator removed water from the grass to give them a more accurate measurement. Here Brent's research assistant gets ready to weigh a sample on the digital scale (on the shelf next to the dehydrator).

Elkhorn Slough sea otters forage for the largest, meatiest crabs first.

OTTERISMS

SEA OTTERS SAVE KELP FORESTS TOO!

Outside of Elkhorn Slough, sea otters also live among kelp beds in and around Monterey Bay *(below)*. Kelp provides many of the same functions as seagrass. It stores carbon, calms waves, and provides a safe place for young fish to mature. After sea otters were hunted to near extinction for the fur trade, sea urchins multiplied unchecked in kelp forests along the western coast of the United States and Canada. These spiny animals feed on living kelp attached to the rocky seafloor (kelp are algae and don't have roots like plants). Giant kelp forests of the North Pacific suffered.

Once sea otters returned to the area, though, scientists noticed that sea urchins rarely ventured into the open to attack living kelp. Instead, the urchins hide from otters in rock crevices and make do with floating kelp scraps. Kelp forests are once again thriving and performing their ecosystem functions more efficiently. With more sea otters, kelp forests store more carbon, reduce waves, and provide a safe habitat for larger numbers of fish.

Otters-absent buckets with a large crab had fewer sea hares, more algae, and unhealthy seagrass. Otters-present buckets with a small crab had more sea hares, less algae, and lush green seagrass. The mesocosms confirmed for Brent that sea otters not only ate crabs but controlled the crab population enough to allow sea hares to clean the seagrass. Clean seagrass could thrive even in a nutrient-polluted environment.

Brent was amazed by what the mesocosms had shown. Before sharing his discovery, however, he wanted to replicate his mini-habitat results in the wild. But he needed to control the presence and absence of sea otters, as he did in his buckets. Testing the presence of sea otters would be easy—they were everywhere in the slough. To test the absence of otters, though, he needed to exclude them from parts of the seagrass meadows. Placing otter-proof cages in seagrass beds seemed to be the best way to do that.

A group of ten volunteers helped Brent design and construct the first cage prototype: a rebar frame welded at the joints and wrapped in chicken wire to prevent sea otters from getting in. The cage also had rebar "feet" to anchor it into the soft sediment on the estuary floor. But when the team tested

Scientific fieldwork is expensive. Brent stretched his budget by building homemade devices, such as these cages, with low-cost materials from local hardware stores. Volunteers supplied the welding equipment and the experience.

the cage in the slough, it failed. A sea otter reached under the trap and grabbed the crab inside. "They're smart animals," Brent says. "If there's prey in something, they'll find ways to get in. They chew on line and on buoys. And they're so strong, they could easily yank open a zip tie."

The group tested three additional cage designs before they were satisfied. The final design was still a rebar cube wrapped in chicken wire, but the designers extended the wire both inside the cage and into the sediment. "We made it impossible for the otters to reach inside," Brent says. "This obviously frustrated them, because we saw the otters literally jumping on the cages to get the crabs."

Brent and his team of researchers went to the areas in the slough where they knew sea otters foraged. They placed the cages in ten different groupings on the floor of the estuary. Each grouping had three cages.

The first cage held two large crabs to mimic an environment without sea otters. (Remember: large crabs = otters absent.)

The second cage contained only seagrass and sea hares. Brent wanted to simulate the presence of otters, as he did in his mesocosms. He left out the small crabs, though, to mimic the effect of a lot of otters feeding.

A third cage had chicken wire covering the top, but the sides and bottom were open. Crabs and sea otters could come and go as they pleased. This cage acted as a control to test whether the shade cast by the chicken wire affected seagrass health.

Lastly, a patch of open space acted as another control to see how seagrass fared outside the boundaries of the cages.

The experiment ran for thirty days. Brent and his team of researchers gathered samples of seagrass and counted sea hares and crabs in each grouping. They each logged about one hundred hours in the water in neoprene dive suits, which started to chafe. "My body was covered in rashes," Brent recalls.

Each cage measures 20 inches (50 centimeters) wide, tall, and deep. The metal poles *(near the top of this photo)* were sunk into the mud to keep sea otters from reaching under the cage to steal crabs.

A fat sea hare floats inside one of Brent's cages.

Back in the lab, they weighed the seagrass, the sea hares, and the crabs, much like they had for the mesocosms, and recorded the results. They studied the differences among the cages and the open space.

In cage 2, cage 3, and the open space, areas with simulated or real otters present, the number of sea hares had increased, the amount of algae had decreased, and the seagrass had grown vigorously. Brent found no difference in the health of the seagrass among those three areas, which validated his mesocosm results. His field experiment with real otters produced the same results as his buckets with simulated otters.

Brent was amazed to discover the link between sea otters and the slough's healthy seagrass.

water overloaded with nutrients. Sea otters, the slough's apex predators, eat crabs. Crabs eat sea hares. Sea hares eat the algae on seagrass. Because the sea otters control the crab population, more sea hares survive to do their housekeeping duties. And seagrass stays clean and lush. In scientific terms, Brent discovered a brand-new trophic cascade—a change to an ecosystem caused by a top predator that affects multiple levels of the food chain.

Of course, before long the detective in him asked other questions. Did sea otters help more seagrass grow than ever before in the slough? Could sea otters help seagrass in other estuaries? Would his discovery affect future conservation efforts?

In cage 1, with otters absent, the crabs ate the sea hares, algae grew unchecked, and seagrass once again fared poorly. These results precisely matched Brent's mesocosm results. Without otters to eat the crabs, the seagrass became smothered in algae.

When Brent realized what this meant, a wide grin spread across his face. He'd solved the mystery of the Elkhorn Slough's healthy seagrass. His results proved that sea otters give seagrass a fighting chance in

SEAGRASS SCIENCE

WHAT IS A TROPHIC CASCADE?

Brent discovered a set of cause-and-effect relationships among sea otters, crabs, sea hares, algae, and seagrass. These relationships make up a trophic cascade. *Trophic* refers to the various levels within a food chain. Sea otters are an apex predator at the top trophic level in the Elkhorn Slough. According to Brent's research, sea otters support the health of seagrass by reducing the crab population. The effects cascade down the food chain. With fewer crabs, the number of sea hares increases and the amount of algae that smothers seagrass decreases.

The discovery of this trophic cascade prompted Brent to study other ways that sea otters support the Elkhorn Slough ecosystem. "Striped shore crabs are commonly found in muddy banks on the coast," Brent says. These crabs—a different species from the ones in his experiments in this chapter—burrow into the banks of the slough. Without predators to control this crab population, the banks become so weak they crumble. It's likely that sea otters eat enough striped shore crabs to reduce the number of holes riddling the banks. That helps the banks remain stable. Stable banks prevent the loss of salt marsh habitat, which protects our coastline and provides a nursery for young marine life.

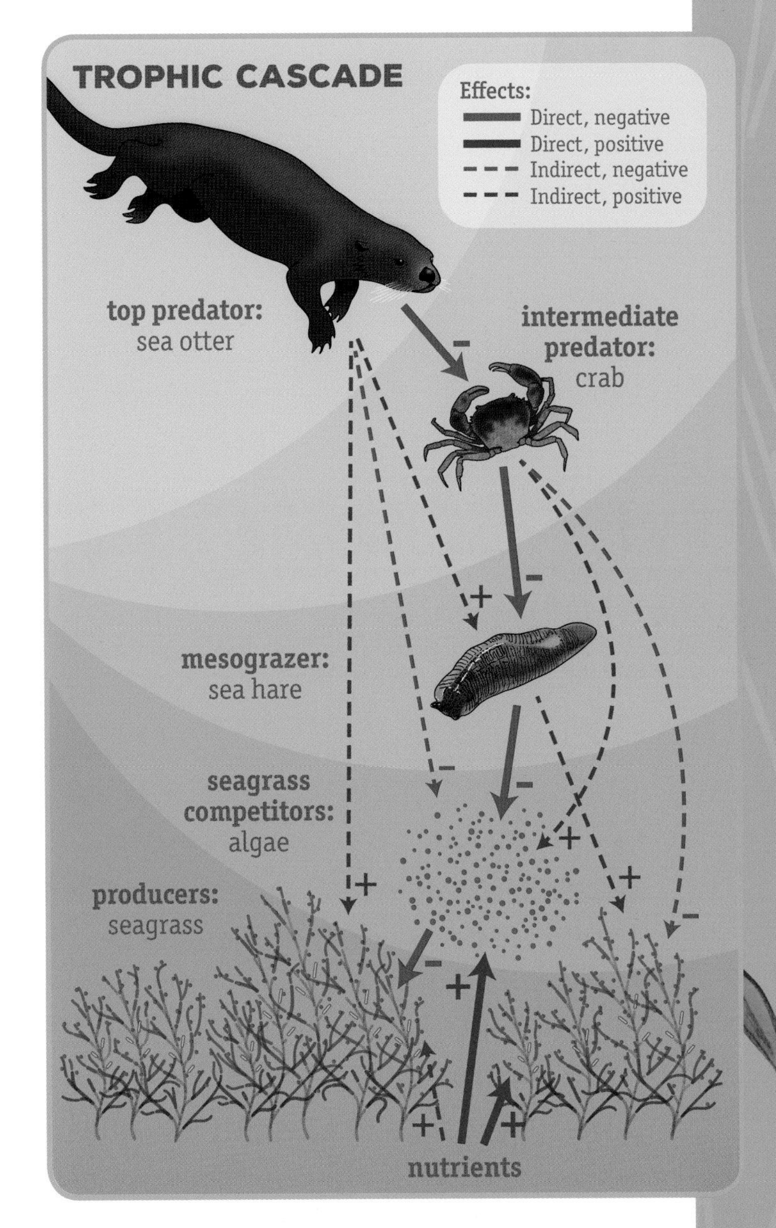

CHAPTER 4

UNEXPECTED HEROES

"WE LIVE IN AN AGE OF RESTORATION," SAYS LILIAN CARSWELL, THE SOUTHERN SEA OTTER RECOVERY COORDINATOR FOR THE US FISH AND WILDLIFE SERVICE, AND ONE OF BRENT'S MENTORS. By the mid-twentieth century, humans in North America had hunted many species to extinction or near extinction, including sea otters, wolves, and whales. People hunted sea otters for their fur. They hunted wolves to protect livestock. They hunted whales for blubber, fuel oil, flexible baleen for women's corsets, and occasionally for meat. Because so many animals were removed from their ecosystems, "generations grew up without knowing what nature was supposed to look like or what was lost," Lilian says.

A gray wolf howls in Yellowstone National Park. In 1923 the last known family of wolves in Yellowstone was killed. Today more than two hundred wolves are once again part of the park's healthy ecosystem.

Ecology as a science took off in the second half of the twentieth century, and it keeps getting more sophisticated. Prior to the 1960s, most scientists didn't study food chains and how species interacted within them. Many didn't yet understand the significance of overhunting top predators.

Eventually, awareness grew. Citizens spoke up and shared their concerns about overhunting with the political leaders who represented them. Politicians listened. Congress passed the Marine Mammal Protection Act of 1972 and the Endangered Species Act of 1973, two radical and far-reaching laws that recognized the value of preserving biodiversity for its own sake.

Thanks to these laws and similar ones in other countries, we're beginning to see

OTTERISMS

WHAT IS NATURE SUPPOSED TO LOOK LIKE?

After the fur industry nearly wiped out sea otters, their prey multiplied rapidly. Entire California fishing industries formed around these prey species, a sea snail called abalone and the sea urchin. When otters returned to their native habitat and their natural prey, the fishers blamed otters for ruining their fishing grounds. They wanted the otters removed. But conservationists wanted sea otters to have access to their prey. Sea otter habits had come into conflict with human habits and jobs.

The conflict raises some important questions. Are the rights of people who make their living from fishing more important than the rights of people who want to preserve marine life? How do the rights of a sea otter, which only eats shellfish, compare to the rights of a human who can fish for any kind of fish? Were the abalone and urchin fisheries unnatural because the original top predator was missing?

a rewilding, or rebound, of many apex predators around the world. "With their return, scientists are coming to realize how much [these animals] contribute to the resilience of their ecosystems," Lilian says.

For instance, Brent's discovery that sea otters act as guardians of seagrass has sparked interest in how top predators may affect other estuaries around the world. Scientists from southeastern Alaska, the Gulf of Alaska, and British Columbia, in Canada, contacted Brent about his experiments. "We are establishing a network of researchers to look at the role of sea otters across their range," Brent says. They expect that northern Pacific seagrass ecosystems might also benefit from the return of sea otters.

Brent's next step is to look at the functions that seagrass performs. "For example, with healthier seagrass" he says, "do we get more fish in the nurseries? Do we get more carbon storage? Can we conclude that we'll see benefits over the rest of the sea otter range? Sharks, cod, and grouper eat at the same level of the food chain as sea otters. Can we conclude that these predators will also benefit their ecosystems?"

If we protect a marine habitat and allow apex predators to return, will damaged ecosystems heal themselves?

BRENT'S PATH TO SCIENTIFIC DISCOVERY

JUNE 2001: Brent graduates from college with a bachelor's degree in biology.

JUNE 2007: He earns a master's degree in marine science.

FALL 2010: Brent starts his PhD studies.

EARLY 2011: He observes that seagrass is flourishing in the slough.

FALL 2011: He requests Yohn Gideon's sea otter data.

MAY 2012: The mesocosm experiment begins.

AUGUST 2012: The field experiment begins.

SEPTEMBER 2013: The results of experiments are published.

DECEMBER 2014: He graduates with a PhD in ecology and evolutionary biology.

Sperm whales release plumes of feces (poop) near the surface. Scientists believe these plumes support a rich ocean ecosystem.

And will they be able to produce more fish for us to eat, store more carbon to clean our air, trap more pesticide-laden sediments, and calm rough seas to protect our coastlines? Brent hopes to answer these questions, and he aims to do the detective work to test these hypotheses.

Many scientists are excited by other suspected trophic cascades. For instance, the Japanese fishing industry sometimes blames whales for reducing the population of available fish. In fact, studies show that when the number of whales decreases, so does the number of fish. Why? Many scientists believe that whales swim at the top of a trophic cascade and affect the existence of species below them in the food web.

Whales affect their food chain by acting like industrial-sized mixers. For example, humpback and gray whales plow wide rifts through sand and shells on the ocean floor to search for food. Long-buried nutrients escape and rise to the surface. Seabirds feed on these floating snacks. After the whales eat their fill, they surface to take a breath and release waste. Colossal explosions of poop, rich in nitrogen, iron, and ammonia, cloud the water. These nutrients help phytoplankton grow, the microscopic plants that make two-thirds of the oxygen we breathe. Phytoplankton attract zooplankton, fish, and seabirds. Predators such as cod and grouper eat the smaller fish. And the ecosystem thrives.

Trophic cascades occur on land too. When wolves were hunted to near extinction in North America to protect livestock, this hole in the food web paved the way for explosions in the deer and elk populations. Large bushes and trees nearly disappeared because the hungry hoofstock gobbled them up before the plants could mature.

In 1995 and 1996, Yellowstone National Park reintroduced wolves to the ecosystem. This triggered a series of changes. Wolves preyed on elk and deer. Fewer deer and elk led to more mature trees, such as aspen and cottonwoods. Trees stabilized riverbanks and reduced erosion. Large trees also welcomed songbirds and beavers, which built dams with branches, stones, and mud. The dams provided attractive habitats for river otters, fish, reptiles, and ducks. Wolves also killed coyotes. A smaller population of coyotes encouraged rabbits and mice to move in. The rodents enticed hawks, weasels, and foxes. Mature bushes once again produced berries, which attracted bears. The return of wolves to the food web healed the ecosystem.

New trophic cascade discoveries hint that we do not yet fully understand how ecosystems work. The near extinction of sea otters, whales, and wolves most likely endangered an entire series of relationships in each animal's ecosystem. "In my view," Lilian says, "Brent's discovery goes well beyond the immediate sea otter/seagrass trophic cascade. It suggests how much we don't know about what we've eliminated by killing top predators." According to Lilian, we must learn to coexist with these predators, rather than killing them. She urges us to "rethink wildlife management as the management of human activities, not the management of animals themselves."

Brent's trophic cascade discovery shows that the recovery of top predators such as sea otters may ensure that seagrass meadows stay healthy, producing oxygen and benefiting people worldwide. His follow-up studies show that the seagrass in Elkhorn Slough not only thrives but expands across the estuary floor thanks to the presence of otters. "In areas of the slough with more sea otters, the seagrass grows more rapidly," he says. "These areas never had seagrass before and are potentially benefited by the otters."

Brent and colleagues jokingly call the Elkhorn Slough the cosmic center of the universe because it's a perfectly contained ecosystem. The apex predator ranges through a relatively small area, and its habits encourage scientific study. Researchers have recorded data on seagrass and water quality in the area for many decades. Even tourists who gather data on their boat tours benefit the scientific community.

The Elkhorn Slough changed the direction of Brent's scientific career. It forced him to take a closer look at seagrass ecosystems and reconsider how species affect one another. By following the clues he found, he discovered that sea otters allow seagrass to survive—and even thrive—in a stressful environment overloaded with nutrients. And that, in turn, benefits the entire ecosystem. Brent may have discovered the link, but the sea otters are the heroes.

SEAGRASS SCIENCE

MAKING A MESOCOSM

Find out the benefits of trophic cascades firsthand. Conduct your own experiment to see how a spider influences your neighborhood ecosystem.

Materials

- plastic PVC pipe, about 2 inches (5 cm) in diameter
- grass with roots attached
- 2 hardware store buckets or large fish tanks with mesh covers
- dirt (enough for each bucket to hold at least 4 inches, 10 cm, of dirt)
- 10 herbivores (grasshoppers or crickets)
- 1 predator (a spider)

Instructions

1. Insert the PVC pipe into your lawn or a grassy area you have permission to use for your experiment, and take a "plug" of grass. The pipe ensures that the same amount of grass is planted in each mesocosm.
2. Spread dirt about 4 inches (10 cm) deep on the bottom of each bucket. Plant the grass plug in the dirt. Water the grass until the soil is moist but not soaked.
3. Insert 5 herbivores into each bucket.
4. Add a spider to one bucket, but not the other.
5. Cover the mesocosms so the animals cannot escape. Make sure to make airholes in the covers.
6. Place your buckets near a window or outside. Plants need sunshine to grow.
7. Count the number of herbivores in each mesocosm every day for two weeks. Water as needed.
8. At the end of the two weeks, compare the two mesocosms. Is one healthier than the other? Why? Do the results change with different kinds of grass?

RETHINK YOUR RELATIONSHIP WITH WILDLIFE

What does it mean to reconsider how we coexist with top predators and vital ecosystems? We need to dump our environmentally unfriendly habits and adopt new ideas that protect the environment. Here are eight ways you can do your part:

- Read about nature. Share what you read with family and friends. Help motivate them to love and defend the natural world.
- Support the natural recovery of native apex predators, such as the sea otter. Raise money in school to support top predator conservation research. Visit wildlife sanctuaries, rehabilitation facilities, zoos, and aquariums to learn more about wildlife. Find out how you can volunteer with those organizations.
- Ranchers and farmers may oppose reintroducing apex predators because the predators kill their cattle or their livestock. Study these challenges, and think creatively about ways to reduce conflicts among humans, their property, and wildlife.
- Many wildlife species become endangered when their habitat is lost. Support natural habitat restoration at nearby waterways. Learn to recognize invasive plants, and advise your family not to use these plants for landscaping. Speak out with posters, videos, and speeches when a natural habitat is at risk. Join river and ocean cleanups.

Students in the Dominican Republic participate in an Earth Day cleanup of invasive plants in a wetland habitat.

- Support tunnels and overpasses to allow native wildlife to find their way across our highways.
- Encourage your parents to use organic fertilizers. They release more slowly than chemical fertilizers and are not easily washed away during watering or rainstorms. And skip the pesticides! Instead, use natural pest controls.
- Don't use single-use plastics, such as plastic bags, straws, and water bottles. They pollute our waterways and kill marine birds and fish. Use shampoos, facial cleansers, and toothpastes that are free of harmful plastic microbeads.
- Learn by observing nature carefully. Brent demonstrated the need to let go of fixed ideas when observations contradicted them. Think deeply. Go past the first step to find the second, third, or fourth step to explain the natural world.

Boyan Slat *(above)* was only seventeen when he invented the Ocean Cleanup floating barrier *(black hanging object, pictured)* to clear plastic from the ocean. His TEDx talk went viral, and he raised over $2 million for his foundation, the Ocean Cleanup. He plans to deploy his device in the Great Pacific Garbage Patch in the near future.

In a shallow lake, these students are able to observe a watery ecosystem up close.

SOURCE NOTES

4–5 Brent B. Hughes, interview with the author, May 6, 2015.

5 Ibid.

6 Hughes, interview with the author, November 19, 2015.

7 Ibid.

8 Ibid.

10 Ibid.

11 Georg Wilhelm Steller, *Journal of a Voyage with Bering, 1741–1742*, ed. O. W. Frost, trans. Margritt A. Engel and O. W. Frost (Stanford, CA: Stanford University Press, 1988), 145.

11 H. C. Bryant, "Sea Otters Near Point Sur," *California Fish and Game*, 1, no. 3 (1915): 135. http://www.biodiversitylibrary.org/item/53391#page/52/mode/1up.

13 Hughes, interview, May 6, 2015.

13 Hughes, interview, November 19, 2015.

16 Ibid.

18 Ibid.

19 Ibid.

20 Ibid.

20 Hughes, interview with the author, November 20, 2015.

20 Hughes, interview, November 19, 2015.

22 Hughes, interview, November 20, 2015.

24 Hughes, interview, November 19, 2015.

29 Ibid.

30 Hughes, interview, November 20, 2015.

31 Ibid.

33 Ibid.

36 Hughes, interview, November 19, 2015.

36 Hughes, e-mail to the author, May 6, 2016.

36 Hughes, interview, November 19, 2015.

39 Hughes, e-mail to the author, February 9, 2016.

40 Lilian Carswell, e-mail to the author, April 17, 2015.

40 Carswell, interview with the author, May 16, 2015.

42 Carswell, e-mail to the author, February 1, 2016.

43 Hughes, e-mail to the author, February 5, 2016.

43 Hughes, interview, November 20, 2015.

45 Carswell, e-mail, April 17, 2015.

45–46 Ibid.

46 Hughes, interview, November 19, 2015.

GLOSSARY

algae: simple plantlike organisms that often grow in water. Algae can cause problems in seagrass ecosystems.

apex predator: the top animal in a food chain

carnivore: an animal that feeds on meat

climate change: long-term changes in weather patterns. Scientists believe climate change in recent years is due to high levels of carbon in the environment.

correlation: the relationship of two things that increase or decrease together

ecosystem: a group of organisms that share a habitat

estuary: an aquatic ecosystem area where freshwater and salt water meet

habitat: the natural home of a plant or animal

herbivore: an animal that feeds on plants

hypothesis: a scientifically testable theory

intertidal zone: an area of the coastline that is covered by water at high tide and uncovered at low tide

kelp: a type of algae in the ocean that grows in cold coastal waters. Areas of this seaweed form a sort of underwater forest.

mesocosm: a laboratory environment that re-creates nature in a bucket, barrel, or tank

nutrient: a substance that provides nourishment for growth

pesticide: a chemical used to kill pests that damage crops

phytoplankton: microscopic single-celled marine plants that form the foundation of the ocean food web

rebar: steel rod with ridges, usually used to reinforce concrete

seagrass: a marine plant that looks like grass that grows in coastal areas around the globe

sea hare: a type of sea slug that eats algae from seagrass

sediment: stones, sand, or other living and nonliving particles carried by water or wind into rivers and oceans

slough: a meandering channel of water

tide: a daily rising and falling of the sea due to the gravitational pull of the moon

trophic cascade: a series of interactions among predators and prey that begin at the top of the food chain and move down to the lower levels of the food chain

SELECTED BIBLIOGRAPHY

Baden, Susanne, Andreas Emanuelsson, Leif Pihl, Carl-Johan Svensson, and Per Aberg. "Shift in Seagrass Food Web Structure over Decades Is Linked to Overfishing." *Marine Ecology Progress Series* 451 (2012): 61–73.

Bryant, H. C. "Sea Otters Near Point Sur." *California Fish and Game* 1, no. 3 (1915): 134–135.

Caffrey, Jane M., Martha T. Brown, W. Breck Tyler, and Mark Silberstein, eds. *Changes in a California Estuary: A Profile of Elkhorn Slough*. Moss Landing, CA: Elkhorn Slough Foundation, 2002.

Carswell, Lilian, interview with the author, May 16 and November 19, 2015.

Carswell, Lilian P., Suzann G. Speckman, and Verena A. Gill. "Chapter 12: Shellfish Fishery Conflicts and Perceptions of Sea Otters in California and Alaska." In *Sea Otter Conservation*, edited by Shawn Larson, James Bodkin and Glenn VanBlaricom, 333–368. Amsterdam: Elsevier, 2015.

Department of the Interior. Endangered and Threatened Wildlife and Plants; Termination of the Southern Sea Otter Translocation Program; Final Rule, Washington, DC: National Archives and Records Administration, 77 Fed. Reg. 244, December 19, 2012.

Estes, James A., John Terborgh, Justin S. Brashares, Mary E. Power, Joel Berger, William J. Bond, Stephen R. Carpenter et al. "Trophic Downgrading of Planet Earth." *Science* 333, (July 15, 2011): 301–306.

"Here's the Scoop on Chemical and Organic Fertilizers." Oregon State University Extension Service, April 30, 2008. http://extension.oregonstate.edu/gardening/node/955.

Hughes, Brent B., interview with the author, May 6, November 19 and 20, 2015.

Hughes, Brent B., Ron Eby, Eric Van Dyke, M. Tim Tinker, Corina I. Marks, Kenneth S. Johnson, and Kerstin Wasson. "Recovery of a Top Predator Mediates Negative Eutrophic Effects on Seagrass." *PNAS* 110, no. 38 (September 17, 2013): 15313–15318.

Levy, Sharon. "Predators Can Help Restore Damaged Coastal Ecosystems." *BioScience*, October 31, 2015, 1–6.

Loomis, John. *Economic Benefits of Expanding California's Southern Sea Otter Population*. Defenders of Wildlife, December 2005. http://www.defenders.org/publications/economic_benefits_of_expanding_californias_southern_sea_otter_population.pdf

Mancino, Joseph, owner, Elkhorn Slough Safaris, interview with the author, November 18, 2015.

Monbiot, George. "For More Wonder, Rewild the World." *TED Talks*, July 2013. https://www.ted.com/talks/george_monbiot_for_more_wonder_rewild_the_world?language=en

Nickerson, Roy. *Sea Otters: A Natural History and Guide*. San Francisco: Chronicle Books, 1989.

No Otter Zone. DVD. Directed by Nicholas DaSilva, Clint Reynolds, and Mark Romanov Spencer Bruttig. Produced by Blue Horizon. San Francisco: Video Project, 2013.

Paine, Stefani. *The World of the Sea Otter*. San Francisco: Sierra Club, 1993.

Raimondi, Peter, L. J. Jergens, and M. T. Tinker. "Evaluating Potential Conservation Conflicts between Two Listed Species: Sea Otters and Black Abalone." *Ecology* 96 (November 2015): 3102–3108.

Riedman, Marianne. *Sea Otters*. Monterey, CA: Monterey Bay Aquarium, 1997.

Ripple, William J., James A. Estes, Robert L. Beschta, Christopher C. Wilmers, Euan G. Ritchie, Mark Hebblewhite, Joel Berger et al. "Status and Ecological Effects of the World's Largest Carnivores." *Science* 343 (January 10, 2014): 1–11.

Roman, Joe, M. M. Dunphy-Daly, D. W. Johnston, and A. J. Read. "Lifting Baselines to Address the Consequences of Conservation Success." *Trends in Ecology and Evolution*, 30, no. 8 (June 2015): 299–302.

Roman, Joe, James A. Estes, Lyne Morissette, Craig Smith, Daniel Costa, James McCarthy, J. B. Nation, Stephen Nicol, Andrew Pershing, and Victor Smetacek. "Whales as Marine Ecosystem Engineers." *Frontiers in Ecology and the Environment* 12, no. 7 (September 2014): 377–385.

Slade, Suzanne. *What If There Were No Sea Otters?* Mankato, MN: Picture Window Books, 2011.

Steller, Georg Wilhelm. *Journal of a Voyage with Bering, 1741–1742*. Edited by O. W. Frost. Translated by Margritt A. Engel and O. W. Frost. Stanford, CA: Stanford University Press, 1988.

Terborgh, John, and James A. Estes, eds. *Trophic Cascades: Predators, Prey, and the Changing Dynamics of Nature*. Washington, DC: Island Press, 2010.

"Two Big Benefits of Using Organic Fertilizer." *SustainAbility Newsletter*. Last modified July 18, 2012. http://www. thesustainabilitycouncil.org/benefits-of -organic-fertilizers. html.

US Fish and Wildlife Service. Appendix C: "Final Evaluation of the Southern Sea Otter Translocation Program, 1987–2012." Final Supplement Environmental Impact Statement on the Translocation of South Sea Otters, Ventura, CA: US Fish and Wildlife Service, Ventura Fish and Wildlife Office, 2012.

Wilmers, Christopher C., James A. Estes, Matthew Edwards, Kristin L. Laidre, and Brenda Konar. "Do Trophic Cascades Affect the Storage and Flux of Atmospheric Carbon? An Analysis of Sea Otters and Kelp Forests." *Frontiers in Ecology and the Environment* 10, no. 8 (October 2012): 409–415.

MORE YOU "OTTER" READ AND WATCH

BOOKS

Davies, Nicola. *The Promise*. Somerville, MA: Candlewick, 2014. This picture-book tale shows the significance of the natural world and why it's important for us to have a relationship with it.

Eszterhas, Suzy. *Sea Otter Rescue*. Berkeley, CA: Owlkids Books, 2016. Take a peek inside the Alaska SeaLife Center for a behind-the-scenes look at rescuing and rehabilitating sea otters.

Kaye, Cathryn Berger, with Phillippe Cousteau and EarthEcho. *Going Blue: A Teen Guide to Saving Our Oceans, Lakes, Rivers, and Wetlands*. Minneapolis: Free Spirit, 2010. This book provides readers with the tools and inspiration to save our waterways.

Newman, Patricia. *Plastic, Ahoy! Investigating the Great Pacific Garbage Patch*. Minneapolis: Millbrook Press, 2014. Journey into the open ocean to explore the Great Pacific Garbage Patch with three female scientists. Find out how plastic is harming marine life and what we can do about it.

WEBSITES

Become a Citizen Scientist with Reef Check
http://reefcheck.org/
Student divers twelve and older can qualify to become citizen scientists and collect underwater data for scientific studies.

Elkhorn Slough National Estuarine Research Reserve
http://www.elkhornslough.org/education/students/index.htm
Visit this site for more information about the slough and for fun activities, puzzles, and wallpapers for your devices.

"George Monbiot: For More Wonder, Rewild the World"
https://www.youtube.com/watch?v=8rZzHkpyPkc
Watch a fascinating talk, from TED (technology, entertainment, design), about how apex predators affect the health of their ecosystems.

Monterey Bay Aquarium
http://www.montereybayaquarium.org/
Watch the aquarium's sea otters on a live web cam. Learn more about the aquarium's sea otter rescue program.

"No Otter Zone"
https://vimeo.com/52140920
This short report tells how the fate of sea otters is linked to sea urchin fishers.

Sea Otter Anatomy
http://oceantoday.noaa.gov/seaotteranatomy/
Check out this excellent introduction to the adaptations that make sea otters successful predators.

INDEX

ABOUT THE AUTHOR

Patricia Newman *(center)* is the author of several books that connect young readers to scientific concepts in the news, such as *Plastic, Ahoy! Investigating the Great Pacific Garbage Patch*, a Green Earth Book Award winner; and *Ebola: Fears and Facts*, a *Booklist* Editors' Choice selection. In her free time, she enjoys nature walks, the feel of dirt between her fingers in the garden, and traveling. She lives in Northern California with her husband. Visit her at www.patriciamnewman.com.

PHOTO ACKNOWLEDGMENTS

The images in this book are used with the permission of: © Color Brush/REX/Shutterstock (seagrass); © Inna Ogando/REX/Shutterstock (waves); © Hotshotsworldwide/Dreamstime.com, p. 1; © Ron Eby/Elkhorn Slough National Estuarine Research Reserve, pp. 3, 8, 38, 49; © David Courtenay/Oxford Scientific/Getty Images, p. 4 (top); © Elise Newman, pp. 4, 6 (right), 13, 14, 15 (all), 23 (all), 28 (top); © Suzi Eszterhas/Minden Pictures, p. 5; © Ed Reschke/Stockbyte/Getty Images, p. 6 (left); © Brent Hughes, pp. 7, 30, 31 (all), 32, 33 (top), 35, 37 (all); © Laura Westlund/Independent Picture Service, pp. 9, 16, 21 (bottom), 24, 39; © Keith Ellenbogen, pp. 10, 19; © Look and Learn/Illustrated Papers Collection; American/Bridgeman Images, p. 11; © 2016 Joseph Mancino/Elkhorn Slough Safari, LLC/www.elkhornslough.com, p. 12 (all); © Rodrigo Beas, pp. 17, 20; © Suzi Eszterhas/Minden Pictures, p. 18; © Mint Images/SuperStock, p. 21 (top); © Lilian Carswell/U.S. Fish and Wildlife Service, pp. 22, 46; © Don Johnston/All Canada Photos/Getty Images, p. 25; © Steven J. Kazlowski/Alamy, p. 26; © Francois Gohier/VWPics/Alamy, p. 27; © Joe Tomoleoni, p. 28 (bottom); © Norbert Wu/Minden Pictures, p. 29; © Gerry Ellis/Minden Pictures, p. 33 (bottom); © David Courtenay/Oxford Scientific/Getty Images, p. 34; © Chase Dekker Wild-Life Images/Moment/Getty Images, p. 40; © SilksAtSunrise Photography/Alamy, p. 41; © Frans Lanting Studio/Alamy, p. 42; © Biosphoto/SuperStock, p. 44; KEVIN SULLIVAN/Orange County Register/Newscom, p. 48; © Michel Porro/Getty Images, p. 49 (top); © Hero Images/Getty Images, p. 49 (bottom).

Front cover: © Michael Quinton/Minden Pictures; © Inna Ogando/REX/Shutterstock (waves); © Color Brush/REX/Shutterstock (seagrass).